Understanding the
LINE OF SUCCESSION

WHAT'S UP with Your Government?

Amie Jane Leavitt

PowerKiDS press.
New York

Published in 2018 by **The Rosen Publishing Group, Inc.**
29 East 21st Street, New York, NY 10010

Cataloging-in-Publication Data
Names: Leavitt, Amie Jane.
Title: Understanding the line of succession / Amie Jane Leavitt.
Description: New York : PowerKids Press, 2018. | Series: What's up with your government? |
    Includes index.
Identifiers: LCCN ISBN 9781538323281 (pbk.) | ISBN 9781538322321 (library bound) |
    ISBN 9781538323298 (6 pack)
Subjects: LCSH: Presidents--Succession--United States--Juvenile literature. | United States.
    Constitution. 25th Amendment.
Classification: LCC KF5082.L43 2018 | DDC 342.73'062--dc23

First Edition

Developed and Produced by Focus Strategic Communications, Inc.
    Project Manager: Adrianna Edwards
    Editor: Ron Edwards
    Design and Composition: Ruth Dwight
    Copy editors: Adrianna Edwards, Francine Geraci
    Media Researchers: Adrianna Edwards
    Proofreader: Francine Geraci
    Index: Ron Edwards

Photo Credits: Credit Abbreviations: LOC Library of Congress; S Shutterstock; WC Wikimedia Commons. Position on the page: T: top, B: Bottom, C: Center, L: left, R: right. Cover TL: Cecil Stoughton. White House Photographs. John F. Kennedy Presidential Library and Museum, Boston, TR: Andrea Izzotti/S, CL: Carsten Reisinger/S, B: Billion Photos/S; 1 TL: Cecil Stoughton. White House Photographs. John F. Kennedy Presidential Library and Museum, Boston, TR: Andrea Izzotti/S, CL: Carsten Reisinger/S; 4: Cecil Stoughton. White House Photographs. John F. Kennedy Presidential Library and Museum, Boston; 5: LOC/ LC-DIG-ppmsca-37602; 8: Daderot/WC; 9: Everett - Art/S; 11: Architect of the Capitol; 12: Everett Historical/S; 13: LBJ Library photo by Yoichi Okamoto; 14: thatsmymop/S; 15: Everett Historical/S; 17 TL, TR: Everett Historical/S, BL: LOC/LC-DIG-det-4a26205, BR: LOC/LC-DIG-ppmsca-31804; 19, 20: Everett Historical/S; 22: LOC/LC-USZ62-117122; 23: Frontpage/S; 24: Dan Howell/S; 25: Joseph Sohm/S; 27: Courtesy Gerald R. Ford Library; 28: Rob Crandall/S; 29: jiawangkun/S; Design Elements: Nella/S, tassita numsri/S.

Manufactured in the United States of America

CPSIA Compliance Information: Batch BW18PK: For Further Information contact
Rosen Publishing, New York, New York at 1-800-237-9932.

CONTENTS

WHAT IS SUCCESSION?

CHAOS IN DALLAS

On November 22, 1963, chaos and fear rang through the streets of Dallas, Texas. President John F. Kennedy had just been shot while riding in a motorcade. At exactly 1:00 p.m., the grim reality was revealed to the world. The president was dead.

Lyndon B. Johnson, the country's vice president, was rushed to the airport. No one knew if there might be more attacks on the horizon, and the security team didn't want to take any chances. They hurried Johnson onto Air Force One. Before the plane took off, Johnson raised his right hand and took the **oath of office**.

After Lyndon Johnson was sworn in on Air Force One, he officially became the 36th president of the United States. The oath was administered by Judge Sarah T. Hughes. She is the only woman in US history to have sworn in a president.

When a US president is sworn in, they take the oath of office from Article 2 of the Constitution: "I [person's name] do solemnly swear that I will faithfully execute the Office of President of the United States, and will to the best of my ability, preserve, protect and defend the Constitution of the United States."

★ ★

Left Hand on the Bible

Many presidents have placed their left hand on a copy of the Bible when they took their oath of office. This is a symbolic gesture that shows they are making a solemn promise and will be answerable to God if they falter. Bibles are also used in courts of law when witnesses take the stand in a trial. Not all presidents have used a Bible, though. John Quincy Adams and Franklin Pierce placed their left hand on a book of laws. In Theodore Roosevelt's first inauguration, he didn't place his hand on any book. Lyndon Johnson used what he thought was a Bible —but it turned

Theodore Roosevelt's first inauguration (shown here) took place on September 14, 1901, after he was elected 26th president of the United States. He was reelected in 1905.

WHO WILL BE PRESIDENT?

Things were chaotic in the United States following the **assassination** of President Kennedy. A cloud of sadness, fear, and uncertainty hovered over the nation. But imagine how much more confusion there would have been if it hadn't been clear who the next president should be. The country would have been without a leader. As a result, many political rivals would have jumped in to try to take the position, leading to more chaos.

Fortunately, a plan is in place for who the next president will be in such circumstances. This plan is called the **line of succession**. The line of succession is the established order in which US government officials may assume the presidency if anything happens to the current president.

FAST FACT

The first time the line of succession was applied was in 1841, when President William Henry Harrison died from pneumonia that he contracted during his inauguration ceremony. He died after serving for only 31 days—the shortest tenure in US presidential history—and his vice president, John Tyler, became president.

CURRENT LINE OF SUCCESSION

The line of succession has changed through acts of Congress several times over the years. This chart explains the current line of succession.

Succession to the Presidency

1.	Vice President of the United States
2.	Speaker of the House
3.	President of the Senate
4.	Secretary of State
5.	Secretary of the Treasury
6.	Secretary of Defense
7.	Attorney General
8.	Secretary of the Interior
9.	Secretary of Agriculture
10.	Secretary of Commerce
11.	Secretary of Labor
12.	Secretary of Health and Human Services
13.	Secretary of Housing and Urban Development
14.	Secretary of Transportation
15.	Secretary of Energy
16.	Secretary of Education
17.	Secretary of Veterans Affairs
18.	Secretary of Homeland Security

The names highlighted in red are elected officials.

None of these cabinet members (highlighted in blue) are elected officials, but rather are **appointed** by the president and approved by Congress.

WHAT THE CONSTITUTION SAYS

DECIDING WHAT-IFS

Whenever rules are being decided by a group of people, the rule makers generally try to brainstorm as many "what-if" scenarios as possible. That way, any future problems can be resolved before they happen.

In 1787, 55 delegates to the Constitutional Convention met in Philadelphia at the Pennsylvania State House, or Independence Hall. Now known as the Framers of the Constitution, these delegates debated many issues back and forth during their four-month convention. They discussed many what-ifs during this time.

Delegates met in September 1787 in Philadelphia to revise the Articles of Confederation. The revision produced the US Constitution, which the Founding Fathers signed (shown here).

ARTICLE 2, SECTION 1, CLAUSE 6

Several of these hypothetical situations discussed by the delegates had to do with presidential succession. Once they came to a consensus on these matters, they included the resolutions in article 2, section 1, clause 6 of the Constitution. This is the part of the Constitution that talks about the executive branch of government.

What-If Scenarios

WHAT-IF HYPOTHESIS	QUESTION	RESOLUTION
What-if #1	What if the president is removed from office, dies, resigns, or is unfit to serve as president? Who will become president?	The Framers agreed upon a solution to this possible situation. If the president cannot continue in office, then the powers and duties of the presidency will be delegated to the vice president.
What-if #2	What if something happens to both the president and the vice president at the same time? Who will become president?	The Framers decided that if this were to happen, then Congress would decide which officer would act as president until the next presidential election.

An Insignificant Office?

In the Constitution, the vice president's duties are only briefly mentioned. Because of that, the nation's first vice president, John Adams, often felt frustrated with the position. In fact, he even said that the vice presidency was "the most insignificant office" that anyone had ever created. Fortunately, things have changed, and the vice president now has several important roles to play.

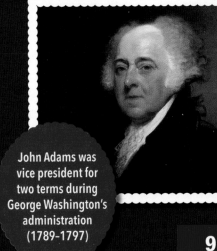

John Adams was vice president for two terms during George Washington's administration (1789-1797)

PRESIDENT-ELECT RULES

There are three places in the Constitution where the line of succession is discussed. The Framers set the groundwork for it in article 2 during the Constitutional Convention.

Much later, in 1933, the 20th **Amendment** was **ratified**. This answered an important question that was not covered in the Constitution and which Congress could not decide.

Here's the scenario. A person is elected president of the United States. But before they have a chance to take the oath of office, they die. Who becomes president? The 20th Amendment solved that problem. It was decided that the vice president would become the president.

Before 1933, this particular amendment was never needed, as no US **president-elect** had ever died prior to taking office. However, the amendment actually did come close to being used less than a month after it was ratified.

FAST FACT

The 20th Amendment also changed Inauguration Day from March 4 to January 20 in the year after the presidential election is held. For example, John F. Kennedy, who was elected president in November 1960, took office on January 20, 1961.

★ ★ ★ ★ ★ ★ ★ ★ ★ ★ ★ ★ ★ ★ ★ ★ ★ ★ ★

On January 23, 1933, the 20th Amendment was ratified. Less than a month later, on February 15, 1933, Franklin D. Roosevelt—then president-elect—was shot at by a would-be assassin. Fortunately, Roosevelt was not harmed in the attempt. Had he been assassinated, his vice president would have taken the oath of office on Inauguration Day.

The man who shot at President-elect Roosevelt was Giuseppe Zangara, an anarchist (someone who opposes all forms of government authority). Roosevelt was saved by an alert bystander who struck the attacker's arm with her purse, deflecting the bullet. But the shot killed Chicago Mayor Anton Cermak instead.

Franklin Roosevelt (center) was inaugurated on March 4, 1933. This was the last inaugural ceremony to be held in March. After that, the ceremonies were held in January.

CONSTITUTIONAL QUESTIONS

The Constitution talks about the executive branch, but many details were left vague. What did the Framers think about presidential succession?

TITLE OF NEW "PRESIDENT"?

Would the vice president be called president, acting president, or still the vice president? The Constitution doesn't make clear whether the vice president would actually *take the office* of the president or just *assume the powers.*

The line of succession debate arose in 1841 when President William Henry Harrison died. The vice president was John Tyler, but many questioned his right to become president. That is why Tyler took the oath of office—to show that he was president. Later, when President Kennedy was assassinated, Lyndon Johnson took the oath of office right away on Air Force One. He didn't want anyone to doubt that he was president.

John Tyler (shown here) was the first vice president to take the oath of office to become president. This became known as the Tyler Precedent.

NEW VICE PRESIDENT?

If the vice president became president, could a new vice president be selected? The Constitution did not say whether the office of vice president should be left vacant. It also did not state how a new vice president should be selected. So for 180 years, in those circumstances, the office of vice president was left vacant until the next presidential election year.

WHO DECIDES?

Who determines whether the president is "unable" to fulfill the duties? The Constitution states that a president be replaced owing to the "inability to discharge the powers and duties of the said office." However, it didn't go into detail. What would happen if this situation were temporary? Could the president resume the powers again? What would an "inability" include, and who would determine it?

Leaving the VP Position Vacant

Leaving the office of vice president vacant could create a leadership crisis. For example, when Lyndon Johnson became president, he was not allowed to select a new vice president. The speaker of the House and president of the Senate were the next in line for the presidency, and they were 74 and 86 years old, respectively. The line of succession was a concern during such a difficult time. No one knew why Kennedy was shot, and the country was in the middle of the Cold War. It was important to have strong leadership.

Lyndon B. Johnson had no vice president until January 1965.

13

THE 25TH AMENDMENT

These particular questions about presidential succession were not matters that Congress could decide through drawing up simple rules or even legislation. They could be resolved only by amending the Constitution.

An amendment addressing these issues had been in the works since 1963. It had been seriously considered since the 1950s. Dwight D. Eisenhower suffered three major medical conditions during his 1950s presidency, and these situations encouraged Congress to start working on an amendment. The 25th Amendment was approved by Congress in 1965 and ratified by three-fourths of the states by 1967.

It took the assassination of President John F. Kennedy (shown here in this painting), on November 22, 1963, for the 25th Amendment to move forward at full speed.

MEANING OF THE 25TH AMENDMENT

SECTION 1: The Tyler Precedent clarified that the vice president wouldn't just act as the president or take on the powers of the president. Rather, the vice president would immediately become the president.

SECTION 2: The country no longer had to wait until the next presidential election year for a new vice president. A way was established for a new vice president to be chosen. The new president would select a vice president. Then, this person would be approved by Congress.

SECTION 3: The president could declare themselves temporarily unable to fulfill the duties of office and give that power to the vice president. Once that inability was gone, the president could assume the powers again.

SECTION 4: The vice president, cabinet members, and Congress could determine whether the president was no longer fit to fulfill their duties. This would happen only in extreme cases and would require a majority vote in order to take effect. The president also has the right to appeal this decision if he or she decides it was made unlawfully.

President Woodrow Wilson is shown here in 1923, four years after he suffered a stroke. He died on February 3, 1924 at the age of 67.

Crisis in Presidential Succession

On October 2, 1919, President Woodrow Wilson suffered a massive stroke that incapacitated him for the rest of his presidency. However, his wife and doctor kept his condition secret from the nation. First Lady Edith Bolling Wilson limited who could see the president and even signed his name to official documents. While she may have felt she was helping her husband while he recovered, she was actually acting unconstitutionally!

A LIVING DOCUMENT

The Framers of the Constitution were skillful in how they drafted that document. Overall, they organized a government that was based on a foundation of solid principles that would stand the test of time. These principles included freedom of religion, freedom of speech, separation of powers, and checks and balances.

The Framers also made sure that Congress could amend the Constitution as situations in the country demanded. This would prevent the Constitution from ever becoming obsolete. By giving Congress the power to make decisions about the line of succession, the Framers allowed the Constitution to stay relevant as the country grew and changed.

FAST FACT

Washington's first cabinet nominee was Secretary of Treasury Alexander Hamilton. He was approved unanimously on September 11, 1,789 minutes after Washington sent his name to the Senate.

Washington's Cabinet

Government was much simpler in 1789. While today there are 16 cabinet members, during Washington's administration there were only four. Thomas Jefferson served as secretary of state; Alexander Hamilton served as secretary of the treasury; Henry Knox served as secretary of war; and Edmund Randolph served as attorney general.

Thomas Jefferson

Alexander Hamilton

Henry Knox

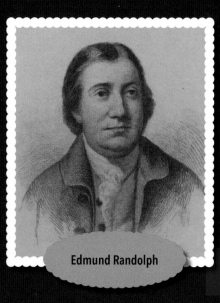

Edmund Randolph

CONGRESS GETS INVOLVED

PRESIDENTIAL SUCCESSION ACT OF 1792

Over the years, Congress passed laws known as presidential succession acts. These laws more fully defined the line of succession. The first such Act was in 1792.

The previous year, Congress began to wonder what would happen if there was suddenly no president and vice president. Who would be next in line?

Many ideas were kicked around before Congress adjourned in 1791. Finally, when Congress reconvened, they decided that the president of the Senate was the third in line. After that came the speaker of the House.

FAST FACT

When Congress did not make a decision about line of succession in 1791, it could have caused serious problems for the country. During this recess, if anything had happened to the president and vice president, there would have been a crisis as no clear successor had been declared.

★ ★

Nearly Implemented

The 1792 Act was nearly implemented three times.

- In 1841, John Tyler became president after the death of William Henry Harrison. Then Tyler was nearly killed by an explosion on the USS *Princeton* in February 1844. He didn't have a vice president, so the president of the Senate would have served as acting president.

- In 1865, John Wilkes Booth and his group planned to assassinate the president, vice president, and members of cabinet. Had they succeeded in their plot and assassinated Vice President Johnson along with President Lincoln, the 1792 Act would have been invoked.

- In 1868, President Andrew Johnson was impeached by the House of Representatives but acquitted by the Senate. If he had been removed from office, the president of the Senate would have acted as president. Johnson did not have a vice president because, as Lincoln's vice president, he succeeded to the presidency after Lincoln's assassination.

John Wilkes Booth is show jumping onto the stage of Fo Theater after assassinating President Abraham Lincoln April 14, 1865.

PRESIDENTIAL SUCCESSION ACT OF 1886

James A. Garfield was inaugurated as the 20th president on March 4, 1881. However, just four months later in July, he was struck by an assassin's bullet. He didn't die right away, but rather lay seriously ill until his death in September.

The line of succession was a concern during these long two months. Chester A. Arthur, the vice president, was also ill. (In 1882 he would be diagnosed with a deadly kidney disease.) According to the 1792 Act, the president of the Senate and the speaker of the House were next in line. But since the 47th Congress was not yet in session, there was no president or speaker. So what would happen if Garfield died and Arthur were unable to take on the duties? Who would be president?

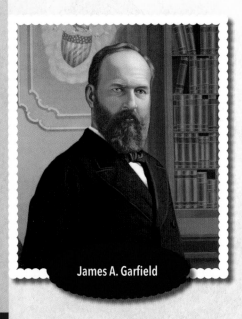

James A. Garfield

Chester A. Arthur

LINE OF SUCCESSION REPLACEMENT ACT

After the 1881 shooting, President Garfield conducted very little official business. The leaders were concerned—who would decide that the president was unable to fulfill his duties?

Garfield's situation sparked a change in the line of succession. In 1886, Congress passed a presidential succession act that replaced the 1792 Act. It removed the president of the Senate and the speaker of the House from the lineup. After the vice president, the next in line would be members of the cabinet, in this order: secretary of state, secretary of the treasury, secretary of war, attorney general, postmaster general, secretary of the navy, and secretary of the interior.

The Presidential Succession Act of 1886

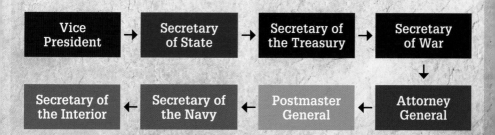

Vice President → Secretary of State → Secretary of the Treasury → Secretary of War ↓

Secretary of the Interior ← Secretary of the Navy ← Postmaster General ← Attorney General

FAST FACT

This question of the line of succession arose several more times in US history until it was resolved when the 25th Amendment was ratified in 1967.

★ ★

PRESIDENTIAL SUCCESSION ACT OF 1947

When Franklin D. Roosevelt died on April 12, 1945, Vice President Harry S. Truman became the 33rd president. He would serve essentially all four years without a vice president.

Truman was deeply concerned about the rules for line of succession. He knew that if anything happened to him, the next in line was his secretary of state. He felt that it was not right that an unelected cabinet member be that close to the presidency.

That was why Truman proposed a revised law in June 1945. He felt that the speaker of the House — who was elected every two years — was more likely to be in tune with the will of the people. So this person should be third in line to the presidency. The president of the Senate should be fourth, followed by cabinet members.

Harry S. Truman was President Franklin Roosevelt's vice president for just 82 days before Roosevelt died. Truman served as president from 1945 to 1953.

CONGRESS AT WORK

Congress went to work to consider the president's proposal. They appointed a special committee to examine it. By 1947, Congress had made their decision, and on July 18, 1947, Truman signed the Presidential Succession Act of 1947. The Act included the lineup as specifically requested by Truman. This is still the current line of presidential succession in the United States.

FAST FACT

From 1841 to 1975, more than one-third of US presidencies ended suddenly because the president died or resigned. The line of succession saved the country from falling into anarchy.

★ ★

Cabinet Member Order

The cabinet members are placed in a specific order relative to the presidency. That order is determined based on when the department that they lead was created. The first departments in the US government were the State Department, the Treasury Department, and the War Department. The War Department was renamed the Department of Defense in 1949.

The Pentagon is the headquarters of the Department of Defense.

CHANGES IN THE LINE OF SUCCESSION

Over the years, there have been changes to the line of succession. For example, the postmaster general was considered part of the president's cabinet and therefore part of the line of succession. However, in 1971, the Post Office Department was turned into an independent agency, the United States Postal Service. The postmaster general was no longer considered a cabinet member and was removed from the lineup to the presidency.

In 2002, following the terrorist attacks on September 11, 2001 (9/11), Congress formed the United States Department of Homeland Security as part of the president's cabinet. Therefore, the secretary of homeland security took the place at the end of the line of succession.

On September 11, 2001, two airplanes hijacked by terrorists struck the World Trade Center towers in New York City. The attacks caused the twin towers to collapse.

SENIORITY OR QUALIFICATIONS

Some people feel that the order of the line of succession shouldn't rest on the date of the founding of the department but on the qualifications of that department's head. For example, the secretary of education is higher in the line of succession than the secretary of homeland security. But it could easily be argued that the head of the Department of Homeland Security would have greater expertise in running the affairs of the executive branch than the head of the Department of Education.

Case of Mistaken Authority

When President Ronald Reagan was shot in March 1981, Vice President George H.W. Bush was out of Washington on government business. Secretary of State Alexander Haig didn't seem to understand the line of succession when he announced on April 2: "As of now, I am in control here..." He apparently didn't realize that the vice president was automatically in charge and that the next two in line were the speaker of the House and the president of the Senate.

President Ronald Reagan survived the assassination attempt. As the 40th president of the United States, he served from 1981 to 1989.

25

SUCCEEDING THE PRESIDENT

THE VP IS A VIP

The vice president of the United States may seem like just the "runner up" to the president. In fact, this person actually has a very important role in the government and in the line of succession. So far in our nation's history, a total of nine vice presidents have become president through the line of succession.

YEAR	VICE PRESIDENT	BECAME PRESIDENT BECAUSE...
1841	John Tyler	William Henry Harrison died of pneumonia.
1850	Millard Fillmore	Zachary Taylor died from an illness.
1865	Andrew Johnson	Abraham Lincoln was assassinated.
1881	Chester A. Arthur	James Garfield died from wounds he received from an assassin's bullet.
1901	Theodore Roosevelt	William McKinley was assassinated.
1923	Calvin Coolidge	Warren G. Harding died from a heart attack while on a speaking tour.
1945	Harry S. Truman	Franklin D. Roosevelt died from a brain hemorrhage.
1963	Lyndon B. Johnson	John F. Kennedy was assassinated.
1974	Gerald Ford	Richard Nixon resigned.

FAST FACT

Gerald Ford remains the only vice president in US history to replace a president who resigned.

★ ★ ★ ★ ★ ★ ★ ★ ★ ★ ★ ★ ★ ★ ★ ★ ★ ★ ★

An Unusual Presidency

When Richard Nixon's vice president, Spiro Agnew, resigned in 1973, Nixon became the first president to use the 25th Amendment to select a new vice president. He chose Gerald Ford, a member of the House of Representatives. When Nixon resigned the following year, Ford became the first person to serve as president without having first been elected as either president or vice president. He then became the second president to use the 25th Amendment to select Vice President Nelson Rockefeller.

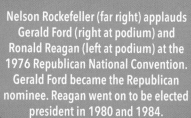

Nelson Rockefeller (far right) applauds Gerald Ford (right at podium) and Ronald Reagan (left at podium) at the 1976 Republican National Convention. Gerald Ford became the Republican nominee. Reagan went on to be elected president in 1980 and 1984.

ACTING PRESIDENT

According to the 25th Amendment, the vice president can also temporarily take the office and duties of president. Since 1967, that has happened several times.

YEAR	VICE PRESIDENT	BECAME ACTING PRESIDENT BECAUSE...
1981	George H.W. Bush	President Ronald Reagan was hospitalized.
1985	George H.W. Bush	President Ronald Reagan was hospitalized.
2002	Dick Cheney	President George W. Bush was sedated for a medical procedure.
2007	Dick Cheney	President George W. Bush was sedated for a medical procedure.

DESIGNATED SURVIVOR

All those in the line of succession often gather in one place for important events. These could include presidential inaugurations or addresses such as the **State of the Union**. What would happen if a natural disaster or terrorist attack took place at the event and no one in the line of succession survived?

This scenario may sound far-fetched, but when you're dealing with security issues and government officials, you can't be too careful. So, it was determined that there would always be a member of the line of succession—a designated survivor—who would not attend any major event in the federal government.

President George W. Bush delivered his State of the Union address on February 2, 2005. His designated survivors for this event were Secretary of Commerce Donald Evans and President of the Senate Ted Stevens.

Two Designated Survivors

At first, presidents had only one designated survivor, or designated successor. But as of 2016, two people are now chosen, and these selections are different for every event. For the 2017 presidential inauguration ceremony, the two designated survivors were President of the Senate Orrin Hatch and Secretary of Homeland Security Jeh Johnson. Designated survivors are always hidden away at a secret location with the "football," a secure briefcase that contains the nation's nuclear codes.

The inauguration ceremony of President Donald Trump occurred on January 20, 2017.

FAST FACT

The television show *Designated Survivor* was based on this exact what-if scenario.

★ ★ ★ ★ ★ ★ ★ ★ ★ ★ ★ ★ ★ ★ ★ ★ ★ ★

GLOSSARY

amendment — a change in wording or meaning, especially in a law or bill

anarchy — the abolition or absence of formal government

appoint — to choose for a job or position

assassination — the murder of a public official

line of succession — the order in which lower-ranking officials may take over the position and title of a higher-ranking official who is unable to continue in that role

oath of office — a solemn promise by a public official to fulfill the duties of the position according to law

precedent — a prior decision or action that becomes the approved pattern for such situations in the future

president-elect — a president who has won the election but who has not yet taken the oath of office

ratify — to give legal or official approval to (as, for example, a bill or treaty)

State of the Union address — a yearly speech given by the US president to Congress and the people to tell them about important things that are affecting the country

sworn in — an event in which an official is placed in office by taking an oath

FURTHER INFORMATION

BOOKS

Hajeski, Nancy J. *The Big Book of Presidents: From George Washington to Barack Obama*. New York: Sky Pony Press, 2015.

Sobel, Syl. *How the U.S. Government Works*. Hauppauge, NY: Barron's Educational Series, Inc., 2012.

Sobel, Syl. *Presidential Elections and Other Cool Facts*. Hauppauge, NY: Barron's Educational Series, Inc., 2016.

TIME for Kids Presidents of the United States. New York: Time Inc. Books, 2017.

Turner, Juliette. *Our Constitution Rocks*. Grand Rapids, MI: Zonderkidz, 2012.

ONLINE

PowerKids Press has developed an online list of websites related to the subject of this book. This site is updated regularly. Please use this link to access the list:

www.powerkidslinks.com/wuwyg/succession

INDEX